Love Loves

Love Loves

J. R. Perry

iUniverse, Inc.
New York Lincoln Shanghai

Love Loves

iUniverse, Inc.

For information address:
iUniverse, Inc.
2021 Pine Lake Road, Suite 100
Lincoln, NE 68512
www.iuniverse.com

ISBN: 0-595-33524-1

Printed in the United States of America

When I begin to count my blessings, I think of you—my dear family—and am reminded of how abundantly rich my life is because of the gift that you are to me. You are another reason I give God thanks. I Love You!

Contents

Love Loves

Introduction

Well as you might have guessed from the title of the book, this is a message about love—a message that has already touched many hearts through something as simple as a poem. That small flame became a huge blaze within the hearts of people who began to understand better what love is and what love does.

One evening while sitting in my living room, I wrote the poem that is the title and overall inspiration for this book. Words began to flow quite easily as I began thinking about the people in my life closest to my heart—those I love dearly—that love is forever embedded within me and shall never fade away.

I shared the poem with some family members and friends. The words provoked positive thought—there were those who asked if they could share the poem with others. Now I have the pleasure and opportunity to share that same poem and so much more with you. I hope the fullness of the meaning of the words presented throughout these pages will find a special place within your heart and be an encouragement and blessing in your life.

It would be wonderful if we could say that everyone is a promise-keeper, but unfortunately that is not the case. There are people who make promises every day that they break. Some say 'I love you' and a few days later they back-track and forget all about how they said they feel—maybe they do not know yet, love is more than a feeling. There are some who do not have a clue as to what commitment means—that is evident because at the first sign of a problem they quickly search for an escape route and dash through the nearest exit door.

It was those observations and words I heard during a church service that inspired the inclusion of some of the information contained within this book. I was sitting in church one Sunday and heard a minister announce that the church was beginning a new program designed to help those who were separated, going through divorce and those whose divorce was already final—the minister called the new program Divorce Care. While it is really an excellent idea to have programs specifically designed to assist those whose family relationship have been broken, I could not help wondering why there was not a preventive program already in place to bring to a halt the ruptures in families by providing valuable training and teaching in relationship care—possibly preventing some divorces from ever occurring. Some relationships fail because people just do not know how to care for anyone else—they do not know the importance of taking care of and valuing what they already have. Sadly, not everyone receives that type of training during their childhood years. A little extra help and training might salvage some relationships. Some people have to be taught what love is and what love does because they do not automatically know.

Love that is authentic is so unwavering that nothing can move it no matter how fiercely it beats against it—well, you will see in greater detail what I mean. Without a doubt, Love Loves.

Some people are trying to amass riches and have totally failed to realize they already have diamonds in their life

Diamonds and Rocks

I heard someone say, "Don't throw the diamonds out with the rocks." The problem some people have is they don't know the difference between a genuine diamond and a rock.

Diamonds are enduring—their value never diminishes. Fire and pressure can be applied to them and they will still be a diamond.

There are people who fit that description—they are diamonds. No matter what comes up in the future and regardless of whatever has occurred in the past, they will always prove to be genuine diamonds—never diminishing in their love, commitment and faithfulness.

Anyone who is trained regarding what to look for can readily identify true diamonds. Sometimes the most valuable of jewels are not found all draped in glamour, surrounded by extravagance. Often diamonds are found among the rocks—sometimes appearing camouflaged by the remnants of dust generated by the rocks, but when the dust, dirt and mud is washed away, the true beauty and value of the jewel is there for all to behold. The inner beauty of a diamond always shows up on the outside for all to see.

Jewels should be taken care of and greatly valued. But not all people realize the worth of great jewels. Some people have not realized yet that they have magnificent diamonds in the form of family members and have been blessed with friendships that have reached diamond status as well. Because they do not know what they have, they sometimes do not treat those relationships with the care that they deserve.

Not very many people are going to throw away their jewels if they know what they have—it is important to comprehend the significance of what you have. All too often because people do not understand the value of what they have, they toss away the diamonds only to be left standing with nothing but rocks—that will crumble at the first sign of even slight pressure.

Learn how to accurately identify the diamonds in your life and to care for them.

Relationship Care Exercise

List the names of the some of the people who are diamonds in your life. Write down at least one way in which they have been a blessing to you. Then make a call or send a note letting them know how grateful you are to have them as a part of your life.

A unified family is a strong and powerful family

A Good Fight

If you must fight about something, make sure it is the right thing to fight about. Now I do not mean take up arms and start fighting with your family and with others creating a typhoon of discord because you believe your way is the right way so everybody else has got to be wrong. I am talking about fighting for those things that are good, righteous, and of lasting value. That would include standing firm and fighting for your family unity—giving family some of your time and attention in an effort to build them up rather than tear them down. That would include fighting to become a better you by utilizing your potential. What you currently are is not all you can become. Utilizing your potential in a positive way to the maximum is what will help you to become the best you can be. That is important to ensure continued growth.

Our view is so limited sometimes—we look at people, form opinions, and draw conclusions about them while all the time thinking we have surely got them all figured out—only to find out later we were wrong. We may not have realized their potential and capabilities, but God knows how to bring out the best in those who are willing to use what they have and start where they are—those who are willing to fight a good fight.

Relationship Care Exercise

So you want to fight? Well, what is there that you want to fight about? Are there any areas within your life that you think could be better and if so, are you willing to fight to make those areas better? List things that you would like to improve upon and be specific about the steps you are willing to take to fight for a better you. Give yourself a specific timeline by which you will start to implement your plan. Review the plan often keeping a written track of accomplishments.

Relationship Care Exercise

Keep on fighting, but this time turn your focus on others—build someone else up. Maybe they only need a kind and encouraging word. Speak words that heal and that help. Make it a deliberate part of your plans to make someone else's day brighter—and do not put those plans off until later. As a matter of fact begin to plan now. You can use this space to write the names of some of the people you would like to encourage. Write specific ways you can make their day a much better one.

*Even the strongest person sometimes
needs a friend to lean on*

Lean On Me

I received a message from family members regarding a hurricane that is projected to strike the city they are currently in. Estimates are that over two million residents have fled their homes seeking shelter in other cities and states. The storm is projected to be fierce creating flooding, downed trees and power lines, and possible structural damage to buildings. Many residents have taken precautions to secure their homes as best they can—and hope for the best.

Out of this seemingly terrible situation have come tremendous rays of love and kindness as people have offered help to others in need—even providing shelter for those who can not find a hotel that has a vacancy, nor find any other place to stay.

There are a lot of things that happen in life that we do not have control over—hurricanes is one of those things. We can not stop the wind from blowing and the rains from falling, but we can refuse to falter in spite of it all.

Everyone has a need to feel they are in a place of safety, that if they lean to the right or the left the walls will not fall down and the foundation will not crumble. They need to know there are people in their life who are unmovable—

they will not run out when times are difficult, but will stand firm. They will be there and even if a flood rolls in, they will not waver nor fear the waters torrent.

It is a good thing to be a person of such steadfastness that you can be someone else's strong tower in their time of need. Can anyone trust you enough to know that they can lean on you and not crash? Have you demonstrated time and time again that you are committed and resolute in your determination to be a person of impeccable integrity—whose word means something? If so, you can say with assurance to family and friends when they are in need, "I am here for you; lean on me."

Relationship Care Exercise

Everyone wants to be able to stand strong and tall at all times, but occasionally may need someone to lean on—somebody to help, somebody to listen, somebody to be there.

If you've ever needed anyone to lean on, make sure you take the time to thank those who were there for you.

If there is anyone in your circle of family and friends who is having a difficult time and you know it, consider how you can assist them. Don't wait for them to come to you, but rather you take the initiative to give them a call and offer help.

*Those who handle
matters wisely find good*

Stabilized

When a person's life is tossed by every wind, stability evades them.

There needs to be some steadiness and faithfulness within every person when it comes to family and friend relationships. We each need to know the gift we have been given in family and friends. Once we understand that, we must determine within ourselves to lift those relationships up with the highest regard—be committed to making them the best they can be.

We do not have to always agree with one another on every issue, but we can still love. To love one another more and more each day is something we should aim for continuously. There is a love that never fails and we need to grasp hold of that same kind of love so that come what may we will always be stabilized. Things might be twisting and turning all around us, but we will remain calm, secure, and firm—unshakable.

Do not be neglectful of family and friends, nor take their kindness and love for granted. Esteem them highly and treat them well.

Relationship Care Exercise

Do you know who and what the gifts are in your life?

How do you treat those gifts—good, fair, bad?

The way you treat others speaks volumes about who you really are within.

Everyone needs a faithful friend—someone who is loyal, committed, and steadfast. Have you been that kind of friend to anyone lately?

Relationship Care Exercise

Do something special for family today—just because you can and just because you want to. Let this be a 'just because' kind of day. Plans to do someone good are the very best types of plans of to make.

There is nothing brighter than
Love's light

Love So Strong

There is strength in love. Love has within it the power to change people, the power to set free, the power to heal those who are broken-hearted, the power to give hope to those who are without hope, the power to turn a life completely around onto a new direction and better pathway.

Just being kind, just showing love can positively impact those who seem unreachable. Love is like an antidote—sometimes when nothing else will help, love is that one thing that can bring about a breakthrough completely turning difficult situations around and changing lives for the better.

Isn't it something that one small thing can have such a great impact on the life of people.

Take the time to exemplify love in action by finding ways to show your family and your friends that you care for them. You might say, "They know that already," but it still won't hurt you one little bit to tell them you care.

It would probably surprise people to learn that there are children who can not remember the last time they have ever heard their parents say, "I love you." There are some parents who can not remember the last time they heard their children say, "I love you." I actually read a story in which a woman stated, "I know my mother loves me, but I have never heard her say it." What a sad statement for anyone to make—no one should have to conclude a statement in the same way. There needs to be a change for the better.

Heal a heart today, show some kindness. Let your family know you care.

Simple expressions of love and simple acts of kindness are all it takes sometimes to wonderfully impact the world one person at a time.

Relationship Care Exercise

People will remember acts of kindness long after the action has been completed. They will remember those who made them feel loved and cared about. So do good things for those you love, but also be verbal—do not let years past without your family hearing you tell them that you love them. So what if they already know it—sometimes they need to <u>hear</u> it.

Love does—
Love is an action word

Just Decide

You have the power to make your relationships, your friendships strong—it is entirely up to you to utilize that power appropriately. God gives us all the freedom of choice.

I remember reading a story about a man who watched in awe at the excitement and genuine happiness of a family who were greeting one another after a brief time apart. It just struck him as unusual and great that a family who had been separated for only a few days would display so much delight about being together again. The man stated he hoped one day to have a similar relationship with his future wife and children. The man was told he could have the same type of relationship—all he had to do was decide. How simple is that—the key to family happiness was not wrapped up in a complicated formula, but rather in a basic decision. Is not that powerful?

The power of decision is really very special. No one can decide for another—there needs to be participation on every person's part to build strong, enduring, and happy relationships. What better place to start than with one's own family.

Some people do not know how much they already have available to them. Some waste precious time turning small things into gigantic mountains, stressing and fighting with those who love them the most—they have decided to fight it out rather than find a way to work it out. They are tearing down, rather than building up.

Keep your family intact and fill your home with an atmosphere of love and happiness—just decide!

Relationship Care Exercise

There are some decisions that should be made promptly. Decide right now that your home is going to be a haven of happiness because you are going to make it that way. Decide you are going to treat your family members like the royalty that they are—just decide. You do not have to wait for anyone else to get their act together. You are not responsible for another person's decision, but only for your own so do your part and the rest will take care of itself. Jot down some of the decisions you can make today that will bring immediate improvement to your life and in your relationships with family and friends.

Wisdom and understanding are both necessary to include in your blueprint for building up and firmly establishing a loving family relationship

At All Times

The sun does not shine every single day. Occasionally, raindrops fall. Likewise in life, there are occasional cloudy and rainy days—times when nothing seems to be working just right and times when we do not know exactly what to do to make everything right. Sometimes all we can do is not allow the circumstances to affect our stance, nor adversely change us in any way.

Someone sent me a message one day stating, "Nothing seems to be working or moving." She had become very frustrated by circumstances that were out of her control—decisions other people in higher positions were making that were affecting her career and life. It seemed she was locked in a never-ending spiral of uncertainty. She was left waiting for the circumstances to change with no clue as to when that would happen. Finally, she realized that even if nothing changed on the outside, she would be alright within—she determined to let go of the worry and maintain a positive attitude.

There are going to be some good times and some bad times. There will be times when circumstances aren't lining up with your desire, but rest assured God is still in control and you shall see the clouds pushed back out of the way, the rain will stop falling and the sun will shine again.

That same person who said to me, "Nothing seems to be working or moving," later shared good news about how her circumstances had changed for the better. It will for you too; just keep on trusting and believing in God to help you.

Be someone who stands firmly even when the rain is falling so the people in your life do not have to wonder if you are going to be around as the stormy weather rages—then they will know your anchor will hold fast because it is totally secured.

There was a woman whose husband was in an accident that left him badly burned and disabled. Some people, including his parents, encouraged her to leave him. All of those people who advised her to leave thought they had to give permission for her to feel okay about going on with her life. They did not want her to feel obligated to hang on in there during the bad times, but she could not be persuaded to abandon her husband. The love the woman had for her husband as well as his love for her taught others what love looks like and how to love. Their love was a source of strength that helped them both through a difficult time. Their future together was full of hope, not sadness—they focused on the blessing they had in one another and in their family.

Are you the kind of person who will be there for family and friends in times of need—times that are difficult? Don't allow the circumstances to change you. If there absolutely must be a change, you change the circumstances—as much as is within your power to do so.

Stand firmly at all times!

Relationship Care Exercise

Be There! Is there somebody who needs to know you are there for them? Let them know you will stand with them for as long as they need you to be there. Is there somebody who needs an encouraging word? If so, don't wait for someone else to come to the rescue; you speak words that will build them up.

Your Worst Day

Sometimes there are days when from start to finish things seem to go wrong on every side. When nothing seems to be able to make a difference, it is amazing how one kind word fitly spoken or one simple deed of goodness can derail what was becoming our worst day.

A friend was fired from her job not because she had done anything wrong, but because the company was down-sizing. Trying to find another job in a similar salary range proved futile. She was highly skilled and trained, but that was not working to her advantage as easily as she had originally thought it would. Someone who knew her well and realized her potential for greatness spoke a word that changed her life when he suggested she start her own business—and she did.

It turns out what was first viewed as being the worst day of her entire career became her best day. She said later, "I never would have started my own business if I had not gotten fired." The income from her own business far surpasses the salary she was making when working at the company that fired her.

Starting her own business and making it a success was a lot of work, but she was blessed to have supportive family and friends with her every step of the way providing encouragement and help from the beginning of what was first perceived to be her worst day throughout each day thereafter.

Some people run for cover and hide when the worst or what they think is the worst starts happening. They will not stand side by side with those in need. But if they only would do so, their actions of kindness, of support, and of love would turn someone's worst day around for the better.

Remember, no storm last forever. The clouds must move. The sun shall shine again. Do not give up.

Relationship Care Exercise

Look around at your circle of family, friends, and co-workers—is there anyone that you can clearly see is having a bad day, a bad week, or even a bad month? Is there a word that you can speak or a kind action you can put into operation that will help? If so, do not hesitate. Write down specific people that you can help and specific ways that you can help them.

*A word fitly spoken
can change a person's life*

Do Your Best

It is easy to look at others and see what we perceive as being their flaws. Sometimes we focus so much on what someone else is not doing that we can not see where we have missed it. Then there are times when we feel that because someone else did not do what they should have done that we are excused from doing what we should do.

There are people who will go so far as to argue with God and tell him all the reasons why they refuse to do their best—usually the most compelling reasons they can come up with is to point out what somebody else did not do.

Some people just need a good example to follow. They need to see what the best looks like. They need to observe people who are doing their best.

Do not mirror another person's actions when you know they are not giving their best efforts to the task at hand. Determine to set a better example and let your standard rise to a level of absolute excellence.

Be responsible, do your part even when others are not doing theirs. That is something you can do in the workplace and at home. Do the best job you can. Develop the best friendships you can.

In all that you do, remember to let love start at home with your own family and give them your best. Love them as they are and if there is any changing that needs to be done, let God make the change.

Relationship Care Exercise

Do a self inventory and take note of whether or not you have been doing your best in promoting love and harmony in your relationships with your family and friends. Be honest with yourself. If you see that you have missed it even by a small level, make it your mission to turn that completely around. Do your best. No one is asking for more. If you will do your best, it will inspire others and encourage them to do their best also.

*You simply can not go
wrong by doing what is right*

No Hidden Agenda

Be considerate and let your only motive be that you have a desire to show another person kindness.

Kindness should not be a rarity, but in the life of some people they can not remember the last time a genuine kindness was shown to them.

Just a few years ago, there seemed to be a considerable increase in people participating in bestowing upon others gifts that they preferred to categorize as random acts of kindness. There were drivers who paid tolls for drivers behind their vehicles. When the other drivers reached the toll booth, they were told their fee had already been paid by the driver up ahead. There were restaurant customers who paid for meals for other customers. When they requested their bill, they were told it had already been paid in full. Some people came up with other creative and wonderful ways to show kindness to others. The effect was dynamic upon both the givers and the recipients. People often talked about what was going on because it was so special to have someone show a kindness for no other reason than just to be kind.

There was a family that was having a difficult time financially. Some people who knew about it decided to give them food and financial help. Their only request was that one day if the family ever saw someone else in need that they would pass the same kindness on. That kind deed had such a tremendous impact upon the family and sure enough a day came when they could pass the deed on.

If you are going to help somebody, do it because you want to. If you say you care for people, show it and let there be no hidden agenda.

Plan to do your family good, to do your friends good, and to do others good. Those are the best type of plans to make. Doing good things for others does not just impact the recipients of your deeds, it will greatly impact your life as well.

Relationship Care Exercise

There are so many opportunities to help people in this world, but sometimes people are wary of accepting assistance and they rightfully should be if they know there are strings attached. If you see some good you can do in your community, your business, your family, or some good you can do for a friend, get busy in helping, but let there be no hidden agenda. Make someone else's day by surprising them in a wonderful and unexpected way.

*Love really listens and
wants to understand and care*

Listen

We can talk so much that we do not hear what the other person is saying. We can get so busy that we do not hear the sounds all around. We can miss out on the biggest blessing because of failure to listen.

Part of caring for others is listening to what they have to say—being attentive to what matters in their life.

Communicating is so vital to building closer relationships, yet people sometimes allow that important building block to slip off balance.

You can not really know and understand another person until you listen to them.

One of the most frustrating things ever is when someone has something to say, but can not get anyone to listen. Just taking the time to listen would stop a lot of misunderstandings from ever occurring.

Have an interest not only in what you have to say, but also hear, listen to what others are saying. If a person feels that you are not listening to them, they will eventually stop trying to talk to you.

One of the greatest compliments you can give a person is to take the time to genuinely listen to them. It indicates that you deem them and what they have to say as being of importance.

Realize the value of quietly, intently listening to what others have to say and when it is your turn to speak, share your views and then listen again. Have a real conversation that allows for all parties to be heard.

I believe most people really want to communicate effectively, but good communication cannot occur if everything is lopsided and slanted—in other words, it is okay to talk, but you have got to balance that off by taking the time to listen to the one you are talking to. I call it active listening—giving your undivided attention to really hearing what the other person has to say. It is so much more interesting, plus you gain a greater insight and understanding of the topic of discussion as well as learn more about the one you are talking and listening to. That can only happen when you are willing to not only speak, but also listen.

Relationship Care Exercise

Beginning today determine to listen more carefully to what others are saying—especially those who are family.

Sometimes when people complain about the infrequency of your calls or your lack of spending much time at home, it may be that what they are really saying is, "I miss you. I would like to talk with you and spend time in your presence." Some of the things we consider as being complaints are not that at all, but we will not know it unless we really listen.

Take the time to listen to what others are saying to you and to what you are saying to others.

Are your words edifying—are they making your situation better?

Are you fully hearing what others are saying to you? Listen.

Whatever a person sows,
will eventually be reaped

Take Action

Anybody can talk and make a sound, but it is really action that makes the difference. We can talk consistently, but until we back up what we are talking about with action, our words are lifeless and without power.

We can say all day we care about people, but if we never help, we never show kindness, we never have anything good to say to them or say about them, our words really have lost their effect.

Sometimes it is the people closest to us who feel the least cared for because we forget to honor our words at home. They may feel that everything else and everyone else is getting our attention except them. We need to take action to ensure they know how important they are to us.

When there is a breach in communication or some misunderstanding arises somebody has got to take action to fix that situation otherwise it is just going to get worst. Sometimes the longer a person puts off trying to repair whatever is broken, the more difficult it becomes to fix the problem.

Anyone who sits back and does nothing will reap nothing because that is what they have been sowing. Take action; sow some seeds of love and kindness.

Allow your words to mean something so that the people who are a part of your life will know assuredly that they can trust in you.

Relationship Care Exercise

Identify those areas in which you need to take action.

If you have made promises to family and friends, but have failed to fulfill them, then begin to take action. Let them see that your words can be relied upon and will not falter.

If you have goals that you have put on the back-burner, then begin to take action in a very clear and measurable way so that you can see progress take place that will bring you closer each day to reaching your goals.

If you want to make your situation better you have got to take action. If you want to achieve your goals and see your dreams come true, you have got to take action. Begin now.

*Any relationship that is built upon
a foundation of conditions is
bound to crash*

Without Conditions

A conditional foundation is a very shaky foundation to build upon. It is virtually impossible to construct a lasting, solid structure or enduring relationship on an uncertain foundation. Some things have to be defined and made clear from the beginning in order to be made strong enough to withstand all that will try to come against it in the future.

A person could actually feel as if they are skating on thin ice that is subject to breaking at any moment if they know you will only stand with them and be there for them based upon a list of conditions.

Just like the weather conditions change, life conditions, circumstances, and situations are subject to change at a moments notice.

Conditional guarantees have as much worth as empty promises when it comes to building sound friendships and family relationships.

If you are going to be there for your family and friends, then just be there and take the conditions off—so that they can have confidence you will not sway, not be moved by the circumstances and situations of your tomorrows.

The circumstances of life will not be able to shatter relationships that are built on solid, strong foundations.

Really take a close look at what you are building your home and family relationships on, at what you are building your friendships on, and at what you are building your hopes and dreams on.

Relationship Care Exercise

Are your family and friend relationships constructed upon a conditional foundation rather than a sure and rock-solid foundation?

Take a real look at whether or not you have placed conditions upon people. Are they fearful of how you are going to react if they somehow miss fulfilling one of your conditions?

Identify what you can do to make your foundation sturdier and enduring.

There is always more to a person than what you see on the surface

Outward Appearances

What are the greatest influences regarding the decisions you make? If outward appearances is anywhere on the list, you might need to consider why that is so. Outward appearances are subject to rapid change.

Outward appearances never tell the whole story so do not let that cause you to miss your blessings.

If you really want to know what is important and real, look beyond the surface to take a look at the heart of a matter and at the heart of a person.

Do not allow appearances to prompt you to retreat and give up on the people you say you care about. The fiercest storm can not rip away those who are anchored to a solid rock—committed and determined.

Only God knows for sure what each day of the future holds, but we can be certain that come what may he holds our future securely and is well able to help us regardless as to how things appear all around.

We need to take God's way of handling situations and circumstances as our example so that we will not give way to defeat when the outward appearance of things seem adverse.

If you need people who are there for you regardless as to what the outward appearances dictate, don't you think there are others who need you be there for them also?

Refuse to allow outward appearances to hinder you from reaching your goals, from making and maintaining good friendships and from being a support for your family even in the midst of a storm.

Look beyond the surface.

Relationship Care Exercise

Do you select your friends based upon outward appearances? For example, do you only socialize with those who appear to be financially prosperous? Do you totally ignore those who do not live up to your idea of what their outward appearance should be?

Outward appearances are important to a degree, but should never be what you base the most important decisions of your life on.

*The most important and enduring
things in life are without
monetary price—genuine love
is one of those things*

Every Person's Dream

Just because we are who we are and do not know everything, we may sometimes make a mistake, but that is not the time to give up, but rather the time to get up and begin again.

Some things fail, but love should never be numbered among them—nor can it be when it is real.

The problem is some people do not know how to define love. They have got it mixed up with something else and they keep thinking that love is failing—but that is not the real cause of confusion at all.

Every person's dream, from a child to an adult, is to feel that they are cared about, wanted, needed, and loved. People need people. If ever that was made crystal clear to me, it was when I heard a 17-year-old student, who had been shuffled from one foster home to another throughout most of his life, state that all he wanted was to be adopted—to have a family. He had never been an official, permanent part of a caring family that he could call his own. A lot of us already have a family and we should not take that for granted for a moment.

One of the goals of every family should be to maintain unity and to have a home that is overflowing with love—a safe-haven that they can go to and feel at peace no matter what is happening everywhere else.

Make someone else's dream come true by being their help in times of need, and being their encouragement in times that are difficult, and being a real friend who truly cares at all times.

Relationship Care Exercise

Identify ways that you can make your home a habitation of love and peace and security.

Identify ways you can more effectively demonstrate your care for your family and friends.

Once you know what to do, then step by step begin to do.

Action is what brings real results.

Just decide to be authentic

Authenticity

That which is authentic is always better than the imitation. It does not matter what category we are speaking about, the real is always preferred instead of the fake.

It does not matter how attractive the fake is or how well-known or well-connected the fake is, nor does it matter how many people think the fake is awesome, that which is real is of the greater worth. The authentic is top-of-the-line, whereas everything else falls below that level.

Often people reproduce jewelry, handbags and other material items to simulate an authentic line of products. People do that when they want to keep their costs down while maintaining the look of the real item that the reproduction is modeled after. In the area of friendship, that which is fake is not acceptable. The costs are extremely high when a person starts settling for imitation friends— the potential for problems to brew are great and are bound to get worst for as long as imitation people continue in their way.

Nobody needs imitation people in their life. Since we all know we do not want imitation friends and relatives, we need to make it up in our mind to be authentic ourselves.

There is no need for authentic people to be altered or changed in any way because they are already of the highest caliber.

No time is wasted in investing in people who are real. It is a complete waste to invest in those who are imitation.

If you want to be part of the best, then be authentic.

Relationship Care Exercise

Sometimes the thing people resist most is being authentic—it seems so much easier for some people to pretend rather than be real.

Decide to be authentic and value those people who are genuine friends.

Just be real—you set the example—let others see in you what authenticity looks like.

*Make your home
a habitation of happiness*

Spread Good Cheer

Have you ever spoken with people who consistently only have a story of doom and gloom to share? They are never happy, never satisfied with anything in life. Their job gets on their nerves, their family gets on their nerves, and their neighbors get on their nerves. They are close to having a nervous breakdown and you will break down too if you keep listening to their negativism.

Those same people get upset and wonder why others seem to be avoiding them. It is just that people get tired of hearing complaints every day.

Those who hear gripes in the workplace or in other places away from home definitely do not want to hear constant complaining when they get home.

Be an inspiration in someone's life—spread good cheer. You might have to work on that at first, but after a while it will become a natural part of you to be positive. Others will notice and it will rub off on and bless them too.

Make your home a habitation of happiness. Take the lead in being cheerful and speaking words that encourage and build up.

Relationship Care Exercise

Is your home a place of good cheer or are you forever griping and complaining? Do your part in promoting cheerfulness. Do not bring doom and gloom in your home. Instead bring in laughter and loads of joyfulness. Shower that on your family. Talk about the good things that are happening. The words you speak can change the atmosphere in your home and make it a much more wonderful place for all who live therein.

When Nothing Makes Sense

It is inevitable that we will encounter situations that seemingly make no sense. People say and do things sometimes without thinking and sometimes they mess up big time—none of that makes any sense.

We can not change other people's actions or determine their responses, but we can make a decision about ours.

There is no reason to accept or put up with nonsense—but however you determine you are going to respond to your particular situation make sure it is the right response. Take time to think. Do not allow nonsense to control you. Your actions can conquer whatever mumbo jumbo is being thrown your way.

Sometimes when people act contrary, the best thing we can do is still be kind to them in spite of their silliness—that will confuse them in a heartbeat. Sometimes, eventually, it will cause them to take a look at themselves and recognize they need to get their act together.

When nothing makes sense, do not despair. No adverse situation remains the same forever. Life gets better.

Relationship Care Exercise

Some people spend a great deal of time trying to change others and eventually they become frustrated when they discover that they can not change another human-being. The only person any of us can change is our self and we can not even do that sufficiently unless we have God's help.

If you have been trying to change other people, cease trying to do so. Instead, leave that up to them and to God.

Completely and Forever

There are some things a person must have a well made up mind about before that person can be completely committed. There is really no such thing as half-way commitment. You are either with it or without it, for it or against it.

If you have ever been wrong about anything, you know what is like to still need to know that you will not be forsaken in spite of the fact that you have been wrong. You might not know where you stand if the people in your life have never exemplified real commitment towards you before your blunder.

Too many people do not know how those closest to them feel about them. They do not have the assurance within themselves of a love that is certain, a love that is complete, and a love that is forever.

How about your family and friends—do they know you are with them all the way—totally committed, faithful, unswerving in your love for them? That does not mean you have to agree with them in all things. There may be times you disagree with them strongly. That is okay. Sometimes disagreement is a good thing because it allows individuals to see another person's point of view—and it might be one that they needed to see. People can disagree about a matter without becoming disagreeable.

Know how you feel about people and what they mean to you and realize how much you mean to others.

Sometimes people can be so selfish—wanting a blessing, but never wanting to be a blessing to anyone else—wanting people to be there for them, but never wanting to be there for anyone else.

We all need people to be there for us. We all need completely and forever people in our life. Those are the best types of people to have as friends and as family.

Relationship Care Exercise

Whether or not people occasionally disagree with one another is not important. What is important is whether or not they handle disagreement the correct way.

Can you honestly say you have been handling disagreements with your family and friends the correct way? Do you know how to disagree without becoming disagreeable—without becoming unkind? Even if it is true that someone else is wrong and maybe that person's actions are the reasons that problems began in the first place, you do not have to follow their lead and be wrong too. You take the high road and do the right thing. Kindness can change even the stoniest heart.

Let love touch your heart
and dwell there

Beyond All Measure

What is the height, the depth, the breadth of love—how can it be measured?

Like the stars in the sky and the grains of sand, real love is immeasurable. We can only comprehend it to a degree, but there's so much more—that is why love grows, and grows, and grows...No matter how many days or years pass by, when it is real, love never stops growing. It is not like a water fountain that can be switched on and switched off. Love flows continually and just like the rain causes the flowers and trees and grass to flourish and the rivers, seas, and oceans to be replenished, so does love bring life and prospers everything and every heart that it touches. Love shoves darkness out of the way and beams radiant light in its place.

Love does not cost a thing—it is a free gift. Bring heaps of love and kindness home. Let it saturate your life and those you care about for always.

Let love touch you and be a part of the person that you are and without fail it will touch those who are a part of your world.

Relationship Care Exercise

Whatever is within a person definitely will show up on the outside at some point. If no one can say you have exhibited any resemblance of kindness and of love, then check out yourself and find out what is going on within you.

Exemplify love in your daily life. Love benefits the giver as much as or even more than it does the receiver; therefore, be love in action for you.

Relationship Care Exercise

Jot down at least five things that you love about the people who are closest to you heart. Would they be surprised by the items you have listed because you have never told them how you feel or why you feel the way you do?

If you are looking for the right moment to say you care, wait no longer because now is the right time to make sure your family and friends know just how you feel

Tell Them

Thank God for holidays. For some that is the only time of the year they express any sign of care for their family and friends. It is certainly not a bad thing to display kindness, love and care during the holidays, but it would be equally as wonderful to display those same expressions throughout other days in the year as well. During the season of the year when good cheer abounds, holiday expressions usually only take the form of cards and gifts. A card and a gift can only say so much, but it can never speak as loudly as words.

There have been people who have stated that they did not have a really good talk with their loved ones until they were very ill and thought they might be on their way out. All of a sudden then it seemed vital to say those things that had for so long been left unsaid.

Do not wait until your health is bad or there is some crisis going on, take a little time out of your day to talk to those who are closest in your life and tell them you love them.

Time does not wait for anyone. Make full use of right now because no one knows what tomorrow will bring.

Relationship Care Exercise

Tell your family you love them. Tell them during the holiday season, but make sure you tell them throughout the year also. Let every day be a celebration of love—you can decide that in your family that is way it is going to be.

Love Loves

The original message and poem, **Love Loves**, was written in March 2001 and shared with a few family members and friends. I learned later some of them passed it on to others. Except for a few sentences deleted from the final paragraph, this is the message and poem as it was originally written.

I was thinking earlier this week about...

...how people sometimes don't take the time to say they care and don't take the time to show it either. It is as if we think we have forever...so we all get so busy with the happenings within our own lives that it just doesn't seem important to focus on anyone else. Sometimes people do or say things that annoy us, things that make us angry, and we don't feel like saying anything nice to them (well truth be told, some of us don't and some of us won't cover another persons rudeness with kindness). But you know what God loves them and us at all times—completely and forever, without one condition. He sees us even in our worst moments and his love never diminishes—'cause Love loves. Does that make sense to you? Well it does to me—so I started writing the notes below...hope you will find them meaningful also.

LOVE LOVES

Love sees the dirt and the mud,
but it also sees beyond the surface…

Love sees the potential…

Love sees what you are capable of becoming

Love knows there is a time when one must hold on,
stand firm and fight,

and Love knows there is a time when one must let go
because it is necessary for your growth

Love refuses to falter, but rather stands firm

Love acts as a tower of defense and
a steady rock upon which one can lean and
be assured of a solid unmovable foundation

Love doesn't change though people change

Love doesn't slip and slide though people may do so

Love doesn't lose its intensity
though it may not always agree
with what you say or do

Love shows up

Love picks up

Love builds up

Love cares

Love shares

Love gives

Love forgives

Love frees

Love opens doors

Love provides strength to those who feel weakened

Love guides and then freely allows you to
make your own decision

Love hears the talk, sees the actions, and
Love loves without missing a beat...

Love just keeps on loving

Love doesn't set itself up to only
make itself known in good times

Love loves even when things have gone bad

Love doesn't change because circumstances change

Love loves

Love can look at you on your worst day and
love you anyway

Love loves even those who don't love in return

Love does not premise its validity on the basis
of another person's actions

Loves takes responsibility and does its part,
does its utmost to do its best
to reach out to you and love you right where you are,
just as you are

Love won't stop 'cause you've stopped

Love won't cancel its plans to do you good
cause you're not sure of what you want to do

Love loves, there's no hidden agenda…

Love won't stop loving you…

Love hears what you're saying and cares about
what you're feeling

Love wants to make your load lighter and
your days brighter

Love wants every good thing you want for you and
so much more

Love won't stand back and watch you hurt and
not try to sooth the pain

Love shows itself in many, many ways

Sometimes Love speaks, sometimes Love just listens,
but always Love expresses itself in action—
sometimes quietly, sometimes loudly
Love cannot help but show itself alive in action

Love doesn't require a list of reasons,
a written notice of why Love should care

Love loves

Love doesn't premise itself upon conditions—
one of Love's cornerstones is that it loves
unconditionally and faithfully

Love may sometimes encounter
things that are disappointing,
but Love never sways

Love hopes, believes, and trusts in God…
knowing he has everything under control
no matter what the outward appearance
of a matter might be

Love can stand and see what it looks like all around and
never buckle, never flinch,
never retreat, never wither,
never allow the storm to blow love away

Love loves

Love is consistent, steadfast, unmovable

Love is a strong anchor, a shelter of safety,
a place where you can rest and not be afraid

Love loves

Love loves you!

Love loves you today!

Love loves you always!

Love never fails

You may fail

I may fail

Things around us may fail

But Love, Love, Love, Love...

won't change its mind, nor its heart about you!!!

Love isn't some recipe that can be altered—
that can somehow be formed into something else
that some other ingredient can act for as a substitute

Love is in a class above all others

Love Loves

Love searches for a new way to make your day

Love gives its best and then prepares
to make its best even better

Love blesses and inspires and spreads cheerfulness
upon every pathway it travels on

Love doesn't put up with nonsense,
but Love knows how to look beyond the
nonsensical happenings and keep on loving

Love doesn't take an intermission,
a time out to figure out whether or not
it is going to continue

Love loves you when you are right and
when you are wrong

Love doesn't love your wrong, but Love loves you...
completely and forever

Love loves

If ever you think there is no one who truly cares,
stop and think again...

You Shall Always Be Loved

God, the one who first thought about Love,

the one who is Love beyond all measure,

won't stop loving you

and I, Yes Me, I have chosen to Love you also,

to Love you dearly, to Love you freely, and

to Love you always

LOVE LOVES

If you have family and friends that you care about, that
you truly love and maybe haven't said so in a while, then
take a moment to tell them. Sure, maybe you believe they
already know (and you could be right), but it doesn't
hurt—doesn't cost a thing—to take the time to tell the
most important people in your life about how you feel
about them. They may need to hear and see it not just on
birthdays, anniversaries, or other special occasions, but
every day. We 'choose' the kind of imprint we leave on the
life of others. So again, those that you love, tell them. Love
loves—completely and forever.

To my family and friends,
I am blessed/honored to know you and
have you in my life

I Love You!

There is nothing greater than Love

In Other Words

1 Corinthians 13 expresses the fact that Love Loves in an even better way because those words were inspired and given to us by the one who is Love. The word charity is used throughout the following verses. Charity is another word for love.

¹ Though I speak with the tongues of men and of angels, but have not charity, I am become as sounding brass, or a tinkling cymbal.

² And though I have the gift of prophecy, and understand all mysteries, and all knowledge, and though I have all faith, so that I could remove mountains, and have not charity, I am nothing.

³ And though I bestow all my goods to feed the poor, and though I give my body to be burned, and have not charity, it profiteth me nothing.

⁴ Charity suffereth long, and is kind; charity envieth not; charity vaunteth not itself, is not puffed up,

⁵ Doth not behave itself unseemly, seeketh not her own, is not easily provoked, thinketh no evil;

6 Rejoiceth not in iniquity, but rejoiceth in the truth.

7 Beareth all things, believeth all things, hopeth all things, endureth all things.

8 Charity never faileth: but whether there be prophecies, they shall fail; whether there be tongues, they shall cease; whether there be knowledge, it shall vanish away.

9 For we know in part, and we prophesy in part,

10 But when that which is perfect is come, then that which is in part shall be done away.

11 When I was a child, I spake as a child, I understood as a child, I thought as a child: but when I became a man, I put away childish things.

12 For now we see through a glass, darkly; but then face to face: now I know in part; but then shall I know even as also I am known.

13 And now abideth faith, hope, charity, these three; but the greatest of these is charity.

Questions for Discussion

1. Along with everything that is real in life, there is always something else that is imitation. People can be the same way—there are authentic people who are real about everything they say and do; then there are imitation people. How can you know the difference?

2. What are your responsibilities in maintaining harmony within your family and within your friendships?

3. What impact does unity have within a family? How is it possible to build stronger, more unified families?

4. Have you ever needed help—needed anyone to lean on? How did you feel about that time in your life? Were there people there for you? How did being on the side of needing help better prepare you to be a person who can help others in the future?

5. Have you ever been around someone who was indecisive regarding important issues? How did their behavior affect their life and that of others?

6. Has anyone else's decisions impacted your life in a big way? Do you consider how your decisions may affect others?

7. There are a lot of hurting people in this world—people who think there is no one who cares. Some of those people come from large families and some from wealthy families. Even though they are surrounded by a lot of people and even though they have riches, they are not happy and do not feel loved. Why do you think that is so and what can be done to make a change?

8. One of the aspects of communicating that people sometimes forget about is that they must not only speak and express themselves, but also listen. Have you ever gotten the impression someone wasn't listening to you? How did you feel about that? Do you think there are times when you do not listen? What steps can you take to improve?

9. How much power do words have—do they really have the capability to build a person up or to destroy a person? How can we strengthen our family by the words we speak?

10. Why do you think there is such great strength in love? What does genuine love have the power to do?

11. Why is loyalty and faithfulness so important?

12. How are relationships affected when a list of conditions are placed upon those relationships? Do you think those relationships can ever blossom and become their best while conditions are in place?

13. How important is it to train children? What are the benefits of training children how to treat others? What are the long-range results of good home training? How can being well-trained as a child help a person when he or she becomes an adult?

14. Do you have a vision for your future—goals or dreams? How will that vision impact your family? Will they be able to contribute to help you achieve your goals and move your dreams into a reality.

15. Are you treating others as you would want to be treated? Are there areas that you think you can improve in and if so, are you willing to take steps that will lead towards improvement?

16. Have you come to a place within your life that you understand that Love Loves? How has that understanding impacted you?

Notes

Notes

Notes

Notes

Notes